LIFE IN A SPIN

*The Riveting Revelations of
an International Helicopter Pilot*

NICK MYLNE

Published in the United States by
Hybrid Global Publishing
301 E 57th Street
4th Floor
New York, NY 10022

Copyright © 2022 by Nick Mylne

United States rights reserved. No part of this book may be reproduced or transmitted in any form or by any means, electronic or mechanical, including photocopying, recording, or by any information storage and retrieval system, without the written permission of the Publisher, except where permitted by law.

Manufactured in the United States of America.

Mylne, Nick
Life in a Spin: The Riveting Revelations of an International Helicopter Pilot
    ISBN: 978-1-957013-00-8
    eBook: 978-1-957013-01-5

Interior design by: Suba Murugan
Copyediting by: Dea Gunning

Published by The Conrad Press in the United Kingdom 2021

ISBN: 978-1-913567-59-0
Copyright © Nick Mylne, 2021

Typesetting and Cover Design by: Charlotte Mouncey,
www.bookstyle.co.uk.

Contents

Prologue	vii
One - A boxing calamity	1
Two - Of joy and of misery	5
Three - Flight school	9
Four - Blue-faced in Aden	12
Five - Echoes at the world championships - Stockholm	18
Six - An unintentional landing and environmental capture	22
Seven - Fire on board	25
Eight - Peeking at the North Sea	27
Nine - Cockroaches over my face - Taif Saudi Arabia	33
Ten - Extended weekends in Jamaica	37
Eleven - The yellow peril	41
Twelve - The wrong side of the law - Iran	52

Thirteen - A terrible start to a project	59
Fourteen - Bleeding meat	60
Fifteen - Oman and the Royal Flight	66
Sixteen - Sultan Qaboos of Oman	73
Seventeen - King Hussein of Jordan	76
Eighteen - Tail rotor failure on a cliff face	79
Nineteen - Arif the thief	82
Twenty - A real mystery	85
Twenty-one - A radical change of plan - Damascus	88
Twenty-two - An incompetent enemy - San'aa, Yemen	94
Twenty-three - Short takes	97
Aeroplanes and helicopters flown	44

Dedication

This booklet is dedicated to my adored and beautiful wife, Dawn.

Prologue

Memories come mostly at random and in isolation. They do not follow a neat chronological order, nor do they tend to include previous and subsequent events. A stressful meeting, a picnic during a particularly happy holiday or a fearful experience, all are complete within themselves.

For this reason, this book follows no sequence – each vignette is a memory plucked at random as they have appeared.

I have had such a wonderful life amongst precious and beloved people, and I hope the reader enjoys these shared moments.

A very special thank you to Peter Loyd who was kind enough to draw the cartoons, and also to Tony Uloth and Scott Wilgrove for their valued contributions.

Nick Mylne – December 2020

ONE

A Boxing Calamity

2 Life in a Spin

Shortly after entering Sandhurst, both I and the Academy realised that it was not a good decision. At the end of my first month I was summoned into my college commander's office to be told I had absolutely no officer-like qualities and – unless a miracle happened within the next three months – he would be recommending my expulsion.

I knew that my mum would be bitterly disappointed and would feel hugely let down, which was the very last thing I wanted to happen. So I decided to make Herculean efforts to stay and looked around for advice. I knew, through the family, a senior cadet and cornered him on his way out from the breakfast hall one morning.

He could not have been kinder and took me aside into an empty classroom. He listened carefully and then explained that the most important factor in assessing cadets was the almighty 'Character Grade.' How it was categorised, he said, was a mystery but it was rumoured that all was well if your character grade was five or above out of the maximum ten. 'Clearly Nick, you have to somehow up your grade.'

'How on earth do I begin to do that Jim?' I asked.

'Well,' he replied, 'It's a gamble, but I am told that if you represent Sandhurst at boxing, two marks are automatically added to your Character Grade. If that is true, it might be enough to put you in the clear.' My heart sank, but I had no choice but to follow his advice.

My entrance into the boxing world coincided with the arrival of a new Academy coach – an ex-professional with unbounded ambition and a total disregard for the welfare of his students. One of the very first matches he arranged was with Oxford University.

Not only was it vital that I performed well, but its importance was magnified as University matches in those days were held in public. We arrived early and sat down as a team opposite the main entrance and waited for the arrival of the opposition. My nervousness rocketed as I watched them file into the hall. They were all huge. However, second from last to enter was a friend I immediately recognised. I got up from my chair and intercepted him before he entered his team's dressing room and asked him to point out to me the person I would be boxing.

'What weight are you, Nick?'

'Welterweight'

'Nick, you are very lucky. The star of our team is our welterweight and he's gone sick at the very last minute so we had to scramble for a stand-in. Come with me and I'll point out your opponent.'

He opened the dressing-room door a couple of inches.

'There – the chap in the red shorts.'

I saw a thin, delicate and narrow-shouldered twenty-year-old. I was elated.

In my imagination I would smash him in the first round, earn congratulations from my Bluebeard coach and start a stunning career on the way to becoming a general.

I almost danced back to re-join my team. However, on the way I passed two young girls sitting in the front row. One was an angel of a blonde and – to my disbelief – gave me a wink and a thumbs up.

I was in heaven.

I was on the eve of a spectacular career and an association with the most beautiful goddess.

I couldn't wait for my turn to fight.

At last, at last my time came up.

I sprang into the ring and, with a heroic eye contact with my divinity, completed a couple of squats in my corner.

I heard the referee call, 'Come into the centre and shake hands!'

With one final glance at her wonderful, wonderful smile, I swung round to face my doomed opponent.

There in the other corner was the biggest gentleman from Nigeria I had ever seen. His stomach was like an accordion, his triceps were almost as big as his biceps – he shone.

And I fainted.

TWO

Of Joy and of Misery

My father died of wounds sustained in the Battle of Knightsbridge in North Africa when I was just five years old. Although my mother spoke rarely of him, I do remember her telling me of his desperation at seeing the two-pound shells from his tank bouncing off the heavily armoured German tanks. The only clear memory I have of him was watching in fascination as he covered his face in soap and shaved.

We lived in Sussex, which was on the path of German bombers on their way to London. Walking to primary school I remember watching the dogfights between the German and British fighters. My brother and I were able to identify the sounds of every aeroplane both German and British. Exciting days.

Two memories have particularly stayed with me: the sound of the air raid warning siren, and the silence of the flying bombs as their engines cut out.

My mother took in paying guests and opened one of the first launderettes in Britain to support the education of myself and my brother. So, at six years old, I was sent to boarding school in Worcestershire where I spent seven wonderfully happy years.

It was paradise. Set under the Malvern Hills, the Quaker school offered its boys so many activities. Carpentry, pottery, nature studies, music, singing, art and five or so different sports.

It even had a miniature railway on which boys with engineering interests worked. Every Sunday we were given long walks accompanied by teachers informing us of the names of the plants, insects, birds and butterflies we came across. The relationship between teachers and students was underscored by both politeness and respect on both sides. The only negative time I remember was having to queue every morning to receive a spoonful of nauseating castor oil.

Too soon it was time to leave, and I was sent to boarding school at Shrewsbury. I have never been so unhappy. Teachers and school boy 'prefects' ruled with total power and without redress. It was possible to receive a caning for the tiniest of misdemeanours, and homosexuality was endemic. When new boys filed into chapel on their first day, should one or two be good looking, they were identified as 'tarts' and were considered fair game.

The ritual for being beaten was pre-historic. Once you were told by a teacher or boy prefect that you were to receive a caning, no action was taken until after you got into bed that night. Then you had to await a senior student coming into the dormitory and announcing in front of the rest of the members that you had to put on your dressing gown and go downstairs. Once downstairs, you had to stand outside the prefects' room – sometimes for over ten minutes – before being summoned to bend over a chair to receive your punishment in front of all the assembled prefects.

Prefects were known by the efficiency of their caning. The worst beating I received was from the captain of the school squash team. He hit me backhand eight times in precisely the same spot.

Prefects also had the power at a whim to summon newcomers to carry out menial tasks such as cleaning shoes, football boots or his study. All they had to do was to stand in the corridor outside their study and shout 'fag!' All juniors then had to run to him and the last to arrive would have to do the job.

Should a newcomer be seen not to comply, it was an automatic caning offence.

My form master was a priest, and one of the subjects in which he specialised was Latin – a subject I found particularly difficult. One morning, he told me to come to his rooms that evening and he would help me catch up on my homework. When I arrived, he apologised that he had no chair for me and that it would be best if I sat on his lap. I fled the room after he started to undo my trousers. I wrote and told my mother who protested to the Headmaster, whose judgement was that both the priest and myself would have to leave the school forthwith.

The thought that I would never ever have to return was just wonderful.

THREE

Flight school

Whether or not Army pilots were destined to fly helicopters or fixed-wing aeroplanes, all students had to complete a preliminary sixty flying hours on Chipmunks. This was a two-seat, single-engine aeroplane developed shortly after the Second World War and was a superb primary trainer.

There were twelve on my course, and our first huge hurdle was to go solo. A really talented student typically went solo after around eight to nine hours' flight instruction. If this hadn't happened by approximately twelve hours the student would go on 'review,' which was the first phase of being rejected.

My instructor was a monosyllabic ex-RAF pilot from Poland. Soon after our first flight together, both he and I realised that I would struggle to make it. The morning of my twelfth lesson dawned and I still hadn't gone on my own. As we climbed into the aeroplane he, amazingly, shook my hand. I had no idea whether this meant an early farewell or was a gesture wishing good luck. After our fourth bumpy landing, he slid back the cockpit and said, 'Go and kill yourself.'

Only one member of my course had absolutely no problems. He was a large, genial sergeant who was supremely self-confident. Solo-ing after only nine hours, he was the first to do the next hurdle, which was the initial solo navigation trip.

Watched by the rest of us, he took his time walking out to the aeroplane, and with a cheerful wave he taxied for take-off. The weather was fine with good visibility and a cloud base of around three thousand feet.

His flight consisted of a three legged track, each leg ending at a prominent landmark and normally taking around forty minutes. After over an hour he had not returned and his instructor initiated the search procedure. Just before the first search aeroplane taxied, the student was spotted joining the landing pattern. When asked what had happened, he told us that he enjoyed it so much, he had added a fourth leg. Unlike his instructor, we students were all so impressed. It wasn't until three or so years later, he admitted to me after several beers what actually had happened.

Apparently the first leg was fine, he identified the initial landmark and shortly after turning onto the second leg he found himself above cloud. Unfazed, he said that he knew how fast he was going, also how long the next leg would take, so all he would have to do was to continue and turn onto the final track for home at the correct time. Shortly before he had calculated when to turn he saw a break in the cloud and quickly descended to see a large ship to his left. He was well on the way to France.

He was so lost and confused that when he turned to look for land he had no idea where he would coast in. Luckily, he recognised Christchurch where he had recently spent a holiday, after which he was able to pick up the aerodrome's homing aid enabling him to return to base.

FOUR

Blue-faced in Aden

When I try and identify what sparked my love of the Arab world – amazingly it was a war.

After qualifying to fly the Army Air Corps Scout and Bell 47 helicopters I was sent to Aden, where the Yemenis were fighting for their independence from Great Britain.

Although, later the fighting spread to the city and to our eventual withdrawal from the country, when I arrived the hostilities were still confined to the mountains around 40 miles to the North of the city of Aden.

I flew for around six months on operations for the Army Air Corps before my regiment arrived and we formed the Air Squadron. This consisted of six Bell 47 helicopters.

Four incidents will always remain with me.

The first was the scandalous way in which night casualty evacuations were conducted. The RAF helicopters were based in Khormaskar, which was about twenty minutes flying time to the operations area.

When casualty evacuation was required, the request initially had to be made to the RAF. During daylight hours this was no problem and the response was efficient and professional. But the local RAF Commander refused to allow his helicopter pilots to fly in the mountains by night. However, he insisted that the initial call for any casualty evacuation still had to be sent through RAF channels. So the wounded had to wait for the call to be refused by Khormaskar, for the RAF to contact the Army requesting a helicopter, for the response to be initiated, and for the flight to arrive in the operational area. This entailed a delay of a minimum of forty-five minutes which, in a number of cases, proved fatal. I remember one night being scrambled to pick up the survivors of an SAS patrol that had been ambushed. By the time I arrived four had died. I shall never, ever forget the hatred in the eyes of their comrades. There was not only no time, nor would there have been any point, to try and explain the reason for the delay.

One of our tasks was to 'call in' the jet fighters to strafe the opposition when identified. The mountains in which the fighting took place consisted of hundreds of deep valleys pitted with numerous caves. The insurgents used these caves from which to operate and to store ammunition.

The problem was to communicate to the fighter pilots as they pulled up exactly the location of the target. So a method was initiated whereby the helicopter pilot flew as close to the target as possible and, as the fighters pulled up, threw a coloured smoke grenade, which was easy to identify from the air and to guide the jets onto the target referencing from the smoke.

The timing had to be exact. Too early, the smoke would have dissipated and too late the fighter pilots would not have had time to identify the target accurately.

Alan, a very good friend, had always wanted to fly and, in particular, to be an active part of an operation. He asked whether he could come with me the next time I was tasked with the role.

Within a week the opportunity appeared when I was asked to confirm the presence of opposition in a cave complex. I contacted Alan, and together we were able to establish that, indeed, there was considerable activity.

As soon as we heard over the radio that the fighters were airborne, Alan asked if he could throw the smoke grenade. I agreed and we waited for the jets to report pulling up. The message came and I told Alan to pull the pin and throw the grenade clear of the helicopter. He tried to pull the pin but was unable to extract it.

By now the fighters had started their climb and immediate action was essential.

Stupidly, I told Alan to keep hold of the grenade and I leaned across the cockpit to grab the ring holding the pin in place. I pulled hard. The pin extracted, and the grenade fell from Alan's hand and rolled under the floor immediately in front of his seat.

Dense blue, acrid smoke filled the cockpit. Vision was impossible. I jettisoned both doors and put the helicopter into a violent side-slip to clear the smoke. With eyes still streaming with tears I was at last able to see enough to keep control of the helicopter.

Having landed we realised that our faces, hands, clothes and the helicopter's Perspex screens were stained an azure blue. The staining lasted more than a week. Soldiers and airmen alike laughingly pointed us out as we passed as the 'two blue idiots' wherever we went.

About six months after the arrival of my Regiment, we hosted the Army Parachute team who came to practice desert drops. As far as I remember the team consisted of eight 'macho' young heroes. Throughout every meal they dominated conversations with stories of derring-do. One young gentleman was particularly sneering in his open derision of anyone who had not the bravery to parachute. The situation became more and more intolerable until at dinner one night, a fellow officer interrupted him half-way through one of his interminable anecdotes saying, 'Anyone can parachute. It really is nothing out of the ordinary.' The young superman rose to the bait and sent out a general bet that none of us would dare make a jump.

I was sitting next to a very great friend of mine, Alex, who was a Beaver pilot. The Beaver was a high-wing propeller-driven, short take-off and landing machine, principally operated as a bush aeroplane. Alex nudged me and said, 'Make him put his money where his mouth is!'

Without thinking I asked him how much he was prepared to bet. Twenty-five pounds - a huge amount of money in those days - was the answer.

To my horror, Alex answered for me and took up the challenge on the condition that we were provided with one of the team's parachutes.

Next morning Alex took me to 7,000 feet above the desert to the north of our base and brought the Beaver to just above the stall speed. I climbed onto a wing strut and jumped.

An experience never to be forgotten.

After the first rush of adrenalin, the parachute opened and suddenly there was silence. I seemed to be stationary in the air. I had just started savouring the wonderful view of the desert and the background mountains when I realised that the ground was coming up – very fast. Except for being dragged by the parachute for around fifty metres on landing before I was able to operate the release harness, the mission was accomplished. Alex and I split the twenty-five pounds.

At a point on the Northern border separating North and South Yemen is Bayhan. If you continue North, you enter the Empty Quarter, and to the West of the town are mountains. I had known the local British intelligence officer since our childhoods. One morning he came to me map in hand and said that he wanted me to take him along the border for a reconnaissance, pointing out on his map the track he wanted us to follow. I compared the route with my map, which showed the border in a thick red line.

'Bill,' I said, 'that track takes us three or four miles over the border.'

With a paternal look he replied that the Intelligence published the border to be three or so miles inside the international borders to ensure stupid people like myself did not come close to crossing. Thus incidents were almost sure to be avoided. Of course I believed him until we were bracketed by three machine guns as I crossed the thick red line on my map.

Dawn and I caught up with him some forty years later in his lovely house on the banks of the River Usk in Wales. When I reminded him of his deception – the reply was a wry smile.

FIVE

Echoes at the World Championships - Stockholm

Echoes at the World Championships - Stockholm

My entrance into Modern Pentathlon was all thanks to a wonderful Physical Training Instructor, Ron Bright, who was attached to my regiment in Germany. He picked me out and encouraged me after I was lucky enough to win the Army Epee Championships, and to briefly become a member of the English fencing team.

The Modern Pentathlon consists of five sports: running, riding, fencing, swimming and shooting.

I had been brought up riding, and my fencing was already up to the mark. Swimming, running and shooting were the areas on which I really had to work.

Swimming (300 metres freestyle) and running (3,000m cross-country) were both hard, hard work and it was just a matter of becoming as fit as possible. Shooting was different, as psychological factors had to play their part. It consisted of .22 calibre pistol snap shooting at twenty-five yards.

In practice I was fine, but the more important the competition, the more my nerves got in the way.

I tried everything - pills, alcohol, counselling, and even diet. With little success.

The World Championship that year was held in Stockholm. The weather was perfect and the first day was the riding competition. We were allowed, a far as I can remember, fifteen minutes to get used to the horse allocated to us and to practice a few jumps before starting the timed cross-country

course. My horse was perfect. She was a lovely chestnut mare, who responded beautifully to the bit, and we had a great round together. A good start.

Fencing (one hit epee) was the next day, and again that went well. One of the very few defeats I had was against a Frenchman, who transfixed me with a hypnotic stare and then hit me on my right toe.

The shooting was held in the most beautiful valley about six miles outside Stockholm. I remember waking that morning telling myself to keep calm. I repeated this mantra time, and time, and time, and time again.

After each exposure, the scores were announced over a loudspeaker, which echoed and re-echoed around the valley.

I still wake up from the nightmare of hearing 'Mintowt-Czar Poland - 98, Williams United States of America – 97, Shultz East Germany – 99, Rialdo Italy – 95, Mylne Great Britain – 5 …5, 5, 5, 5' echoing, and re-echoing, and re-echoing.

SIX

An Unintentional Landing and Environmental Capture

In the studies of aviation human performance, one of the topics is that of 'Environmental Capture.' Once a human being attains a skill, actions begin to be automatic. We learn skills from an early age and they can vary from tying one's shoe laces, or walking up a

An Unintentional Landing and Environmental Capture   23

flight of stairs, to driving a car through dense traffic at night. or a violinist playing a complicated piece of music. The limbs are working without deliberate and conscious thought. Of course, we could not survive without this capability. However, skills do have their weaknesses. One of which is Environmental Capture. During the time a person is conducting a skill, the environment or conditions change, but the actions of the skill are continued inappropriately and do not adapt to this change. On one inauspicious occasion I was a casualty of this phenomena.

From Germany, I travelled back to the U.K. to join the team of flying Instructors at the Army's Central Flying School at Middle Wallop in Hampshire. It was a particularly happy time. All our students were of the finest material, having had to pass the most stringent medical and aptitude tests. This made our job happy, relaxed and, in turn, allowed us to get to know our students to such an extent that many became lifelong friends.

It was a long and glorious summer. For all of June and July, we had clear beautiful skies with, at the worst, puffy fair weather cumulous clouds with endless visibility. I got into the habit of taking my students away from the airfield to carry out the lesson for the day, and on return, over a small coppice about 600 metres outside the aerodrome boundary, switch off the engine so that my student could carry out an engine-off landing. This routine continued day, after day, after day until it had become an automatic act.

Towards the end of July, the environment changed. That morning a twenty- five knot wind sprang up out of nowhere. Otherwise the conditions were exactly the same – wonderful visibility, clear blue sky dotted here and there with the odd little, puffy white clouds. At the end of that morning's lesson, I remained in the automatic mode and switched off the engine over my coppice, unconscious of the wind change, which was in the opposite direction of our approach. This radically changed our angle of descent. We ended up in the middle of a ploughed field short of the airfield boundary. We were unhurt, but hugely and unforgettably embarrassed.

SEVEN

Fire on Board

For a short period of time after the introduction of the Bell 47 into the army, the helicopter was prone to rotor brake fires. Although the brake was small, it was situated below and between the fuel tanks, so prompt action was very necessary if a fire was to break out.

I was tasked to pick up a general and take him to a parade in Northern Germany. He was immaculate, and clearly was very aware of his appearance. You could have shaved from the reflection of his shoes and Sam Brown leather belts. He preened himself in front of the Perspex bubble of the helicopter before boarding. On take-off, we climbed to about 2,500 feet above the ground and levelled out for the hour's flight. When we reached a region close to Hohne, which was used for army exercises, I smelled burning. I immediately landed on a deserted and flat area with not a house in sight.

Here was my chance to show my expertise. I told the general to stand clear of the helicopter as I dramatically grabbed the fire extinguisher. With great élan I pushed the handle. To my horror only a dribble of liquid appeared.

So there we were in the middle of nowhere with a helicopter burning in front of us.

The flames were only small, but clearly were not going to extinguish and the fuel tanks were horribly close. I was desperate, and the only thing I could think of was to climb up and urinate onto the flames. I almost succeeded, but there was still the odd flicker of flame. I turned to the general and said to him that he had to finish it off. Initially he was outraged, but I helped him up and he achieved the necessary.

I couldn't wait for the accident report to be published. I expected it to praise me for lateral thinking and using my initiative to avoid a disaster in losing a helicopter. Might there even be an official commendation?

Finally, it was published - and I was criticised for using corrosive liquid on a helicopter.

EIGHT

Peeking at the North Sea

The early 1970s saw the great expansion of drilling new wells in the North Sea, and for the exploration of new areas as far North as the Hebrides. As the number of oil rigs increased, so did the demand for helicopters to service them. The purchase of new helicopters to meet this demand was relatively straightforward. The problem facing companies was the acquisition of pilots. This proved to be a huge problem, and the Civil Aviation Authority met the challenge by granting temporary licences to pilots holding foreign licences until such times that the pressure eased. At the time I was sent North by the company, a number of American ex-Vietnam experienced helicopter pilots had been recruited.

In spite of the pilot shortage, my company hesitated to transfer me, since elements within the company had the opinion that ex-army helicopter pilots would not be able to qualify to fly in cloud relying solely on the helicopter's instruments to control the flight. Only ex-Royal Air Force and Royal Navy trained pilots were trained to fly under such conditions.

In order to do so, pilots must pass an Instrument Rating. It is probably the most demanding of all the tests a commercial pilot has to face. It consists of a flight of about ninety minutes with an Examiner from the UK Civil Aviation Authority. Throughout the test, the helicopter must be flown extremely accurately regardless of turbulence, strong and changeable winds interspersed with simulated emergency situations. The pilot under test has shades in front of the windscreens so that it is not possible to see out of the helicopter. Everything centres around the helicopter's instruments.

I managed to persuade the company management that I would be able to make the transition and drove to Aberdeen at the end of June. As I entered the city it was snowing – what a welcome!

Having completed my conversion onto the Sikorsky 61N (an approximately thirty-passenger helicopter) the only hurdle left was the Instrument Rating check flight.

The day dawned as a beautiful autumn morning with clear skies and superb visibility. The Government Examiner briefed me and, having boarded the cockpit, he leant over and placed the shades across the windscreen in front of me. I noticed that he had not fixed them correctly and I could still see out of the bottom gap that had been left.

All went well I thought and the finale was an approach onto the main runway at Aberdeen Dyce airport. The vital instrument on which I had to rely had two bars. One showed whether you were left or right of the runway, and the other indicated whether the helicopter was below or above the required glide path. The object was to keep both bars central. I could see the threshold of the runway through the gap that the Examiner had left, and was able to fly a safe approach. Both needles on the instrument remained firmly central as was required.

I felt elated and as I left the cockpit I turned to the Examiner expecting his congratulations. He paused, put his hand in his pocket, pulled out a pen and wrote on his millboard. He tore out a sheet of paper and passed it to me. I read the letters 'YFNKM.' I asked him for an explanation and he said 'You f......... nearly killed me!' In those days, should the instrument fail be activated, both bars showed central. I had forgotten to switch it on.

The weather over the North Sea can be horrendous, especially during winter, but worst of all it can change at the drop of a hat. At the beginning of a flight the wind can be light and then suddenly you can find that you are facing an eighty knot headwind. Not only were we serving oil rigs, but also the associated support ships. Landings onto these were particularly frightening since the helicopter landing pads were always on the extreme stern or bow of the ships. Consequently, in heavy seas the landing areas could be pitching up to thirty-five feet or so. At the same time there was the roll to deal with. Landings at night under these conditions were particularly terrifying.

Of all our tasks, the top priority was the saving of human life and attending to the breakdown of an oil rig. Both had the same priority. Whatever the weather – we went. I still have nightmares of landing on one of the small supply boats to pick up a seriously injured mariner in a snow storm at night. It is one of the few times in my life that I prayed.

The Americans who were given temporary UK licences were all, without exception, amazing pilots. In those early days on the North Sea rules and regulations were few, and these pilots took full advantage of the fact. We had no weather radar on the helicopter, and I shall never forget flying out to a rig near the Shetland Islands with an American pilot. Twenty minutes out we hit thick fog. He descended to about thirty feet over the waves, slowed the helicopter to a near hover and climbed up the side of the rig to land safely on the helipad.

A number of the American pilots lived in flats in the centre of the city and, opening the door to visit, was my first experience of the effects of the pervading cannabis. They were a real tonic and were all to a man optimistic, positive, and a wonderful counterpart to the Granite City and its greyness. We British pilots – after getting over our initial horror at their innovation and creativeness – learnt much from them.

My bank balance during my stay in Aberdeen was even in a worse state than usual, and I was faced with the inevitable: I had to find a second job. Fortunately, I had teamed up with a friend in Germany who had worked as a croupier in a casino in Germany. He had showed me how to gather and count chips quickly and accurately. I was given an interview by the owner of a small casino tucked away in the docklands of Aberdeen. His only interests were whether I was mathematically agile and whether I could manipulate chips. So I found myself working at the tables and also having to commit to the flying roster.

It was a very depressing time. I found it demoralising to watch players lose and lose again, but buoyed temporarily by an occasional win that spurred them to continue. I remember one lady in particular. Clearly not well off, she arrived every evening as the doors opened. Within an hour she had lost all her chips but back she would come the next night, and the next, and the next. When it became clear that I was jeopardising flight safety by trying to burn the candle at both ends and resigned, she was there on my last night at the tables. Nearly four months later I saw her sitting at the corner of a street outside a supermarket with her retriever and begging bowl.

However, there were moments which were pleasurable. Seeing the Northern Lights on the way to the most Northern oil rigs, and the delicious hampers given to us by the rig crews when we flew on Christmas day, completing a difficult landing in very bad weather and, above all, the wonderful camaraderie.

On return from a particularly long flight in miserable winter weather I opened a letter offering me employment in a new organisation flying for the Sultan of Oman and his family.

I almost ran to the post office with my letter of acceptance.

NINE

Cockroaches Over My Face - Taif Saudi Arabia

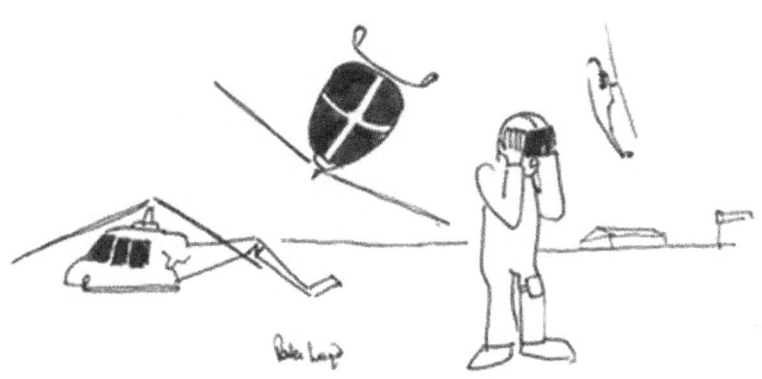

I studied for my Commercial Helicopter licence at Oxford Flying Academy, and shortly before the end of the course I saw an advertisement looking for instructors for a flying school starting up in Saudi Arabia.

The salary offered was stupendous. At the interview in London I discovered that the school was to be run by an Italian company.

Before starting I had to go to Italy to be converted onto the types of helicopter the school were using, which were the Augusta Bell 206 Jet Ranger and the Bell 205.

The conversion took place at the manufacturer's lovely aerodrome in North Italy. The training was wonderfully relaxed, and towards the end I was told that there would be a delay before the Saudi school opened. In the meantime, they expected me to work as a test pilot for new helicopters coming off the production line at the factory at the same aerodrome.

The quality of helicopter produced at the factory was superb, but the efficiency of production often resulted in delays between the time customers were promised their helicopter and the date when the machines were actually delivered. From time to time, customers visited the factory to see how their purchases were progressing and certainly did not wish to be told of delays. I discovered that the problem was overcome in a simple and effective way.

One morning I was informed that customers from a Middle East country were visiting in a couple of days and I was to test fly one of their helicopters prior to the visit. When I walked out to the helicopter I saw that the roundels and colouring belonged to a different country and customer. I was told not to worry about it. On the day of the visit, I saw that the same helicopter I had flown earlier had had the paintwork and roundels changed to those of the visiting delegation's country who were told that this was their helicopter. They were given a superb lunch and left contented.

Eventually I was flown to Saudi Arabia and soon realised why my salary was so high. The flying school was about a ten-minute bus ride from Taif, (a mountain town about fifteen miles East of Jeddah). But there was no administrational backup for us. Unable to speak a word of Arabic, we were expected to find our own accommodation negotiating with the local landlords. Of course they demanded a deposit and the first month's rent in advance. This swallowed our initial salary and we were faced with having to furnish our flats, which were all totally bare. I shall always remember that first month sleeping on a mattress on the floor and being woken intermittently throughout the nights by cockroaches crawling over my hands and face.

Our passports were taken from us upon arrival, and communications back to Italy were through the local Post Office. If there was a problem, we had to queue to send our message, which was translated into Arabic. At some point the Arabic was translated into Italian. If we were lucky, a reply would be received a week later and – because the Italian had to be translated into Arabic and then into English – the answer often bore little relation to what had been our original request.

The school was run by a Saudi colonel – a delightful and accommodating man. But it soon became clear to me that the real power and influence was held by a Captain who was rumoured to have strong connections with the Saudi Security organisation. I warned the Italian management, but they continued to treat the

Captain with distain eventually to their cost. I heard later that the contract was not renewed. The Saudi students were, on the whole, excellent but those few who did not come up to the mark appeared to be impossible to fail, unfortunately.

Because of the lack of support and the difficulty to keep up standards, one by one instructors left and returned to Europe. I was one of the last to leave, by which time I had fifteen students.

My demise came when I was given a student who had not been cleared to go solo, in spite of the fact that he had over thirty hours of instruction, (the average Saudi student would be expected to go solo after about fifteen hours of instruction). I spent hours of extra time with him, but when he had received a total of forty hours' instruction, I told management that he must be failed, otherwise he would kill himself and maybe others.

I was told either I was to send him solo or my contract would be terminated. I chose the latter and returned to England as quickly as I could and, on my return, was fortunate enough as to be employed by Bristow Helicopters based in Redhill, Surrey.

TEN

Extended Weekends in Jamaica

In the middle of an icy German December, I was called into my colonel's office to be asked whether I would be prepared to take part in an exchange with the Jamaican Air Defence Force.

I would spend six months flying with them in Kingston, and some poor and unfortunate Jamaican pilot would have to spend the rest of the winter in freezing North Germany flying with the Army Air Corps.

I packed for the lovely weather of Jamaica and boarded the helicopter dressed in short sleeves and summer trousers. No one had told me that we were to fly via Goose Bay in Canada where we would spend the night. We disembarked into deep snow and a night temperature of minus twenty degrees. I have never been so cold.

The Jamaican Air Defence Force consisted of a number of fixed-wing planes and eight helicopters. I could not have been looked after better, and found myself amid the most charming and generous community of aircrew and engineers. We worked in an atmosphere of total relaxation. It was not unusual for a pilot to take a helicopter home for the weekend returning back to base maybe on the Monday, or Tuesday, or perhaps even the Wednesday.

Engineering practices were novel. Should the centre of gravity be outside the limitations of any helicopter, control becomes impossible. The skids of the Jamaican helicopters were hollow and the centre of gravity was altered by inserting weights and pushing them forwards or backwards. I remember trying to take off one morning and as I lifted up, the helicopter started to move forward, and however far I pulled the stick backwards it made no difference. Clearly the centre of gravity, for some reason, was out of limits. Horrified I complained and was met with a huge smile by the duty engineer, and the skids were opened and the weights pushed towards the rear of the helicopter. I was asked to try again and again until eventually the weights were in a position to allow the helicopter to be controlled. It was all a matter of suck it and see.

The beautiful island was full of contrasts, from wide pristine beaches and fast flowing rivers to jungle with little or no surface water. The most inhospitable part was called, 'Cockpit Country,' which consisted of almost impenetrable jungle. I was told it was a famous refuge in the past for escaped slaves.

I was tasked to support a company belonging to a British infantry regiment, which arrived to spend a month conducting manoeuvres in Cockpit Country.

How or who thought the project up, I have no idea, but I do know that there was no knowledge of the hellish conditions that the soldiers were in for. It could not have been a worse choice for an exercise area. Not only was movement almost impossible, but water was a problem almost immediately and we had to resupply continuously. After about ten days we were told that exercises had ceased and would not be continued.

One of the most beautiful places was Newcastle, which was a collection of buildings tucked away in the Blue Mountains, famous for their production of excellent coffee. Because of its height and ambient temperatures, it posed difficulties when landing and taking off and we used it frequently for training. It has an interesting history.

It became a military centre in the 1840s when Major General Sir William Maynard Gomm, Lieutenant Governor of Jamaica realised that yellow fever, a major cause of death among the British troops stationed in Jamaica, was far less prevalent in the mountains. After unsuccessful attempts to persuade the British government to pay for the construction of a military barracks up in the hills, Gomm went ahead with construction of barracks on his own initiative. The death toll among the troops posted to the West Indies garrison, formerly regarded as virtually a death sentence, declined dramatically.

The day I packed to return to Germany, the avocado tree outside my house began to fruit.

ELEVEN

The Yellow Peril

I was sent to Bristow Helicopters central flying school to convert pilots onto both the WS/55 Whirlwind and the Bell 206 Jet Ranger.

The company was started by Mr. Alan Bristow, a former test pilot for both the Royal Navy and Westland Helicopters. The first company he formed was Air Whaling Limited. In June 1957, he established Bristow Helicopters Limited after securing a contract for the supply of helicopters and crews to support oil rigs belonging to Shell Oil Company in the Persian Gulf. By the time I joined the company it had operations worldwide. The company's services included pilot training, search and rescue, cargo transportation, and charter flights, in addition to its more traditional helicopter transport services. The business had also developed a presence in the North Sea, Middle East, South America, Africa, Asia, India, Bermuda, Trinidad, Australia, New Zealand, The Gulf of Mexico, and Alaska. It was the most remarkable achievement.

This success necessitated a leader with exceptional drive, innovation, determination and supreme self-confidence. Alan Bristow had all these attributes. He was hugely respected and, at the same time, feared by his employees. His word was absolute.

He owned his own private helicopter, which was a Bell 47 and was known as the 'Yellow Peril' after its paintwork. I was called into the Chief Operations Manager one morning and was told that, on top of my normal duties, I was to fly Alan wherever he wished in his helicopter. Whatever I was doing at the time, I had to drop everything and obey the call. At the same time, I was warned that he would want me to be available at weekends to take him to his shooting club situated to the North of Heathrow Airport. Redhill was to the South and thus I would have to cross the dense international traffic landing and taking off at Heathrow. This, I thought, would be no problem as long as I submitted a Flight Plan to Heathrow Air Traffic Control and obeyed instructions. How wrong I was.

One of Alan's pet mantras was that Air Traffic Control existed for the convenience of aircrew. If he wished to cross Heathrow, he would do so and there would be no need to require permission or indeed to contact ATC. My solution was to ask Engineering to install a discrete radio set in the helicopter and every time I needed to contact Heathrow, I turned my head away and looked outside the helicopter so that Alan could not see my lips moving and spoke to ATC. He never rumbled what I was doing.

After flying with him as much as I did, I got to know the family and realised that Alan's overbearing and bombastic manner hid a heart of gold. I was able to witness his reaction towards his employees at times of stress and – when the chips were down – he always fought for and supported the members of his staff. A truly magnificent man.

Aeroplanes and Helicopters Flown

Aeroplanes and Helicopters Flown **45**

Chippmunk

Bell 47

46 Life in a Spin

Bell 206 Jet Ranger

Bell 204

Aeroplanes and Helicopters Flown 47

Bell 205

Bell 212

Hiller

Puma 330

Aeroplanes and Helicopters Flown 49

Super Puma

S61N

50 Life in a Spin

Westland Scout

WS55 Whirlwind

"Images sourced from Wikipedia and printed here under Attribution-ShareAlike 3.0 Unported (CC BY-SA 3.0) with thanks to the originators.

TWELVE

The Wrong Side of the Law - Iran

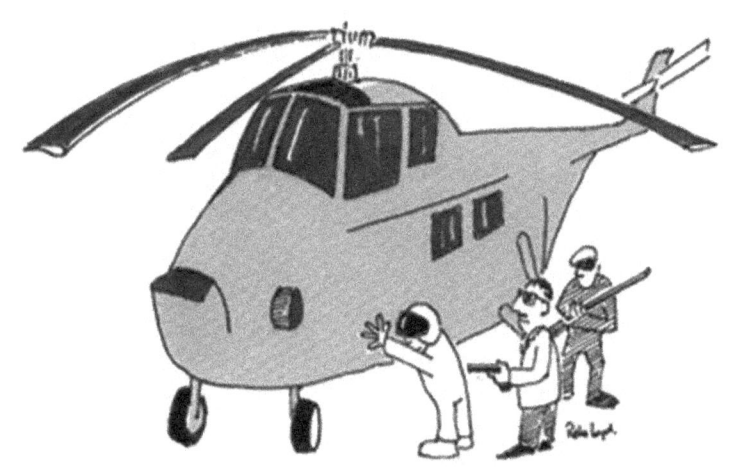

After returning from Saudi Arabia I joined Bristow Helicopters, which was based in Redhill, southwest of London. I was told that my first job with the company would be flying off-shore supporting the oil rigs in the Arabian Gulf.

I was to operate from an island called Levan, but would be living in Tehran. The roster dictated doing fortnightly stints on the island, followed by a week off in Tehran. However, first I would have to do a conversion course onto the Westland's S55. This was a tank of a helicopter with a cockpit high above the passenger cabin area.

Having got the conversion course under my belt, and before being let loose on my own, I had to complete an off-shore familiarisation phase and obtain my local Iranian commercial flying licence. Tehran was a wonderful city – as long as one kept well away from driving.

But best of all, I discovered that about fifty or so miles to the North of the city was the most fantastic ski-ing. However, infrastructure was in its infancy. There was the odd ski-lift, but no medical or casualty services. On a Thursday I had finished the lengthy training, obtained my Iranian licence and was due to fly to Levan on the Saturday for my first fortnight operating on my own. I decided to spend the last day skiing and, travelling with a friend from the British Embassy, we left early on the Friday morning in his Landrover. The weather and snow were perfect and we were almost alone among the most beautiful scenery. Buoyed with enthusiasm for life, I took a turn much too fast, fell and broke my left leg in three places. The hour and a half journey back to hospital in the back of Tony's Landrover over fifth class roads was eternal. It was a month before I could start flying once more.

The company served around eight oil rigs from Levan, and one of my first tasks was to carry out a crew change on a British rig called, Discovery Three. It was at the limit of the helicopter's fuel range and that summer the humidity was so high that a permanent mist covered the sea. The only method of finding the rig was to home onto a notoriously unreliable radio beacon.

That morning the mist was particularly dense, and I knew that if the radio beacon became unreliable, it would be all too easy to fly past the rig without seeing it. If that happened probably the only outcome would have been to ditch. About 10 minutes from the time I was due to arrive the Morse code signal from the beacon went silent in my headsets. I have relived the next ten minutes many times. By the grace of the Lord I did notice a vague shadow to my right - and there it was.

The Westland's S55 helicopter's cockpit was situated well above the passenger compartment. On one trip out to an oil rig for a crew change, I felt the aircraft suddenly behave as if we were flying in air turbulence. The weather was perfect with very light winds. I couldn't fathom what was happening. After three or four minutes everything went back to normal. On landing my crewman told me that he had to intervene in a fight between two of the oil employees.

News came that the company had bought a brand new helicopter – a Bell Jet Ranger – which was to also to be based in Levan supporting a couple of Italian rigs. The Italian rigs were the most popular, as they were the only installations which allowed their workers and visitors alcohol. This magnificent pristine machine arrived on Wednesday afternoon flown by a French pilot. It was quite a different beast from the WS/55. A racing horse compared to a carthorse. Most sensitive of all were the pedals, which controlled the pitch on the tail rotor. With the WS/55 it was common to land on the rig, lock down the controls, and for the pilot to leave his seat to supervise the loading of passengers or cargo with the rotors still running. The French pilot took off the following morning after a bottle of champagne had been cracked over the helicopter landing thirty minutes later on the very small landing pad. Without thinking, he did what was usual with the WS/55. But as he opened the door to exit, his foot touched one of the pedals of the Jet Ranger. The helicopter spun violently to the right, rolled over and toppled into the sea. I was sitting in the Levan Operations Room at the time and heard his now famous call. 'The new helicopter – it is gooorne!'

The WS/55 had cargo space under the passenger cabin floor. The cargo space was rarely used, since to gain access passenger seats had to be removed. Landing one afternoon from a trip to Dubai I was met by four or five Iranian policemen. As soon as I had closed down the helicopter's engines, they boarded and told me and my crewman that we were arrested, and that a search of the helicopter was to take place. As we stood and watched, they opened the cargo space to find it filled with radios, small televisions and cigarettes. To my intense relief, my crewman admitted guilt, identified his accomplices in Dubai and told them that I had nothing to do with the operation. I was un-cuffed and heard no more about it. I gathered later that the Iranian authorities had been watching him for some time.

Another memory stands out. Once in a while we were sent to an island called Kharg, to spend three or four days supporting oil rigs in the area while the current helicopter was either being repaired or serviced. The accommodation was a huge block of bedrooms three stories high housing, I imagine, more than two hundred men working in the oil industry both off and on shore. That summer was particularly hot and humid when I took my turn on the island. A couple of nights after my arrival, we were all woken at around two o'clock in the morning by the building shaking violently. I was thrown from my bed and it took a good five or so seconds to realise that it really was an earthquake. As I headed for the main stairs, we were being thrown from one side of the corridor to the other. And so were the rest of the two hundred of us. Once I was outside, I looked around to see over a hundred stark naked men.

News came that the company has a new contact with the Iranian Airforce, which was opening a new school for young potential pilots on a small airfield to the south of Tehran, and that I was to join the team of instructors. The helicopter on which we had to teach were the early Bell 47 with wooden blades.

Tehran is approximately 4,000 feet above mean sea level so that the air is rarefied, and this is exacerbated by the high temperatures of summer. The combination of a small engine and wooden blades under these conditions guarantees a miserable helicopter performance.

The students had been selected with care and they were a joy to teach. However, there was one exception. A charming young man with elevated family connections, he was enthusiastic, motivated, optimistic and great company. His only problem was that the coordination between his brain and limbs was – at the very best – appalling. Progress was glacial with him, but finally we reached the part on training which precedes going solo, which are 'circuits.' Circuits are merely taking-off, flying around the airfield and landing. They are important insofar as, that to be done properly, the student must have mastered speed, height, engine and direction control, landing techniques, and emergency procedures.

One summer's morning I was downwind to land with Ahmed. He was flying the helicopter and we were around 700 feet above the airfield. A large bird, (I think it must have been a bustard of sorts), flew in front of us and Ahmed, alarmed, jerked at the throttle in his attempt to avoid the animal. At the same time, his left wrist must have turned, and in doing so he stopped the engine. To the left of us was Tehran, with a thousand buildings, wires, obstacles and lots and lots of very hard things to hit. To our right was the open airfield and miles of flat desert.

As the helicopter started to descend, to my horror Ahmed turned the helicopter to the left. We were headed towards a block of flats and all I can remember is a pair of blue spotted ladies pants hanging out to dry on a balcony filling the Perspex as I was able to get the engine restarted to climb away. I have no idea how close we were to the building, but it must have been inches.

THIRTEEN

A Terrible Start to a Project

Once back in Oman from Damascus, my wife Dawn decided to follow her line of research into the Bedouin. The poorest and most isolated of the tribes in Oman at the time was the Harasiis. Living in an area the size of Scotland within the central deserts, they had only one supply of fresh water from a well in a small settlement, Haima. The people relied on the milk from their goat and camels, and the herds obtained their liquid from the seasonal morning heavy dews. The families followed the grazing, and many lived under tarpaulins erected against shrubs. Unlike today, the tribe had no medical, educational, or social government support. They spoke a language derived from Yemen, which was quite different from Arabic and was, of course, unwritten.

Although the language was maintained by the mothers, gradually over the years, Arabic is taking its place mainly as there is now a school in Haima.

Dawn succeeded in creating a co-operative effort between the Ministries of Health, the Interior, Education and Social Affairs and Labour to supply the basic services that the tribe so desperately needed.

She then presented her initiative to the United Nations in New York, asking for financial support in partnership with the Omani Government. Again she was successful and was able to recruit two helpers from the United States Peace Corps.

In order to gain access, and also to win the confidence of the scattered families, she planned to begin a mobile immunisation programme against diphtheria, polio, whooping cough, measles and tetanus. For this they needed a vehicle, a guide, a driver, co-operation from the local Governor, and accommodation from a central location. Radio communications also were essential in case of an emergency, accident or breakdown.

A new Landrover equipped with extra long-range fuel tanks, a high frequency radio set, two extra spare tires, sand tracks and comprehensive spares were all purchased and installed.

The first trip she made was to explain the project to the local Governor of Haima, and to obtain his permission to recruit a guide and a driver, and also to arrange accommodation. Just the two of us made the six- hour drive in temperatures of around fifty degrees centigrade. All went well, and she was assigned a guide by the name of Knadish, who together with his family, over the years, became beloved friends.

Knadish is an expert tracker and is one of the few to know the whole of the tribal area. He was able to gauge the tire pressures of the vehicle by the sound of the escaping air, fix a carburettor in driving sand, capture a hare with his bare hands, and entertain the group with his intimate knowledge of the families and the tribal history.

On the return journey to the capital the same day, we decided to take a break at the only hotel in Nizwa for a drink, refuel and a wash. We had done nearly twelve hours in the vehicle with only an hour's break at Haima. Nizwa is a town about fifty miles south of Muscat. We parked the Landrover outside the hotel next to a small blue car. Dawn went inside for a wash, while I refuelled the vehicle from one of our metal jerry cans. As I poured the petrol into the vehicle, I saw a spark fly between the chassis and the jerry can. The fuel caught alight and I backed away as the whole vehicle and its precious contents went up in flames.

It took a great deal of persuading the local police that I had not been smoking while refuelling, and that the reason for the fire was clearly a build-up of static electricity after our long journey in the heat.

Dawn took the whole debacle amazingly well, and she made sure that the replacement vehicle she bought was grounded.

The only casualty was the little blue car, which we had parked next to. It was made of fibreglass and the whole of its nearside had partially melted from the intense heat. We heard later that it belonged to an employee of an oil company who had quietly taken a day off without permission. It just wasn't his day.

FOURTEEN

Bleeding Meat

The day after the month of Ramadan ends is known in Arabic as Eid Al Fitr –and fasting ceases. Around seven o'clock in the morning in Salalah, I was contacted by the Oman Air Force to ask whether we could help out distributing meat to the front line troops. There was a large attack on some caves to the West, which involved all of their serviceable helicopters.

I was alone with just the Sultan's private helicopter, which was beautifully furnished with velvet seats and a pristine interior. I explained that we could not possibly use his helicopter on such a task without his express permission, and this would take time to obtain even if he was willing to agree. The Operations Officer came back saying that the situation was extremely urgent and unless distribution was known to have been started, the morale of the troops would be severely affected at a critical time. I knew that Sultan Qaboos, if he had been told about the situation, would have been sympathetic and I agreed.

The Air Force produced plastic sheets to cover the furnishings of the helicopter and it took the whole day for myself and my crewman, Saud Mohammed, to fly to over thirty- five front line troop positions. Of course, by the end of the day the raw meat had leaked blood through the gaps in the plastic coverings and the flies were having the time of their lives inside the helicopter. We spent the whole of that night scrubbing and washing the carpets to bring the helicopter back to its original state. Just before turning in I sent a message to the Royal Flight Operations room reporting what had happened that day.

Next morning, I received a message over the radio from the commander of the Royal Flight in Muscat that my behaviour was outrageous and completely unacceptable. My employment was to be terminated as of that morning, and a relief pilot was being flown down that afternoon. I was to start packing.

I knew the first equerry to the Palace well, and fortunately had the telephone number of his private house in Salalah and that he was in at the time. Having explained my problem, he promised to inform the Sultan. A couple of hours later I was told over the radio from Muscat that the relief pilot was no longer to travel.

FIFTEEN

Oman and the Royal Flight

The twenty years I spent with the Royal Flight of Oman are so full of wonderful moments that, as I sit down to write this, I am bewildered how even to begin.

Up until around the middle of the twentieth century, the country was physically and culturally separated from the rest of the Arab world to its north by the band of desert of the Empty Quarter and its extension to the East. Thus its people looked out to sea, and it became a major sea-faring nation and the cultures of India and Africa are still very much apparent. This mix has given rise to an ambience of politeness, tolerance, and huge generosity. There are two expressions one hears time and time again which, to my mind, underscores Omani customs which are: 'My house is your house,' and 'more important than the journey is your companion, and more important than the house is your neighbour.'

When I arrived both the living accommodation and the helicopter facilities and hangers were still at the building stage. The helicopter section of the organisation consisted of a white Bell 212 helicopter for the Sultan, and a Bell 205 for the use of his escort guards.

I was told that wherever the Sultan travelled his helicopter must be immediately available. This was to include his visits to Salalah, where the Dhofar war was still in progress. Thus a trip to the South in order to see what facilities were available was necessary. I was flown to the area by a Polish pilot. When I asked him how long would the flight take, he replied 'Oh, about seven and a half cigarettes.' He had smoked half way through his eighth cigarette as we touched down.

The first obvious problem I noted was the colour of the Sultan's helicopter, which clearly advertised itself as a primary target to the

Dhofar insurgents. Amongst the weapons with which the opposition were equipped were Sam 7 anti-aircraft missiles, so it was clear that something had to be done. The only solution was to cover the helicopter in camouflage- coloured washable paint whenever it was in the Salalah area, and to rinse it off when the helicopter returned to the capital area in the North. Of course after three or four visits to Salalah, the original paintwork was damaged tragically. Added to this problem was that the Bell 212 was very underpowered when it had to operate in a hot and humid environment. Thus it became apparent early on that the helicopter would have to be replaced as soon as it became economically viable.

Muscat to Salalah is approximately six hundred miles by road of which only twenty miles or so were tarmacked. Soon after my arrival, we were told that the Sultan wished to travel by road to Salalah. We were to escort the convoy of around fifty vehicles to lead the way across the central desert, and to provide guidance and an airborne ambulance service if required. The journey was taken at a gentle pace, the Sultan stopping for a couple of days at campsites along the way, which enabled the local population to visit him with their requests and petitions.

The Royal Guard provided the ground security and, naturally, their radio communications were in Arabic. This meant that instructions from the ground to the helicopter had to be handled by the Commander of the Royal Guard who was British. On that first journey I realised that it would be a great advantage for me to learn Arabic.

The first major hurdle was the apparently Sisyphean task of learning to read and write Arabic. I therefore started to try to learn aurally, using language cassettes. This proved to be a huge mistake, as the local dialects pronounced the same word quite differently. This was brought home to me with a vengeance after I had been invited by an Omani friend to visit his family in the countryside and to share a lunch with his parents.

I arrived to find that the meal was set on a long carpet under a beautiful arcade of palm trees and we were among twenty or so guests, many of whom were elderly local dignitaries. My friend and I sat at the end of the carpet - being the most junior. Although I had resolved to speak some Arabic the whole surroundings were so impressive that I lost confidence. At the end of the meal coffee was served accompanied by a delicious sweet jelly called Halwa. I was told by my friend that this was traditional at all Omani meals.

The next time I was invited, I was determined to speak and rehearsed, and rehearsed a sentence about the Halwa, which I knew would be served. We arrived to find twice the number of guests, which included a Governor of a local province. At last the Halwa was being passed from guest to guest and my chance had come. 'Oh,' I said. Conversation stopped and every face turned to me. 'This is delicious,' I continued, 'Is it correct that it is made out of honey, sugar and urine?' There was a horrified silence and then the Governor started to laugh as did the others. I had no idea what I had said, and it was six months later that my friend plucked up the courage to tell me. I had pronounced the word for 'butter' with the incorrect vowel.

The performance of helicopters decreases in hot, high, or humid conditions. Oman had all three. Although the organisation expanded to three Bell 212s, during the first three years of operation, it became clear that a more powerful helicopter was needed to do the job. The decision was made to buy three Puma helicopters manufactured by the French company Aerospatiale at the Marseilles airport of Marignane. Myself and three other pilots travelled to the factory to be converted onto this new type of helicopter, to air test the helicopters once they came off the production line and, all being well, to ferry them to Oman.

All went according to plan and on the morning of our take-off for Oman we discovered in the back of one of the helicopters twelve bottles of champagne, which was a gift from the company to the Sultan. We realised that it would be unacceptable to present such a gift to the Palace. Our route took us from France through Italy, Greece, Rhodes, Cyprus, Saudi Arabia, the United Arab Emirates and Northern Oman. The longest leg of the journey was from Cyprus to Saudi Arabia and fuel might be a little tight should we experience an unusual headwind. On taxi for take-off from Larnaca, we were held up by ATC for nearly twenty-five minutes due to an emergency declared by an inbound air liner. All this time we were burning fuel. As we coasted in, we experienced a forty-knot headwind. I dread to think the number of times I calculated and re-calculated whether we had enough fuel to make it, and I shall never forget the relief we all felt the moment we sighted the first available refuelling aerodrome on the oil pipeline. We had less than ten minutes flying time left.

The aerodrome was run by an oil company and we were welcomed by the few ex-patriate employees, and although we planned to sleep in the helicopter, we were all offered very comfortable and welcome accommodation. Here was an opportunity to rid ourselves of the champagne. We opened a couple of bottles, which we all shared, and gave the rest away to our hosts. Five years later, I flew into the same airfield to discover that I had to produce my passport to a Saudi Arabian security officer. We chatted and he was most friendly until he saw my name. To my amazement he told me that I had behaved very badly in that the authorities knew that I had drunk alcohol five years ago in his country. I was very lucky that he was not placing me under arrest.

Except for hitting a violent and very rare snow storm over Jordan by night, happily the six-day ferry flight was completed without further incident.

The twenty years I spent with the Royal Flight passed in a flash, and it all came to an end most unexpectedly. We were escorting the Sultan on one of his in-country tours and had arrived at a camp site close to the Saudi Arabian border on the edge of the Empty Quarter. Around two in the morning, I woke with a pain across my chest. Luckily the next tent to me was occupied by the Sultan's doctor. I managed to wake him and he diagnosed a heart problem. I was flown to London in one of Qaboos's executive jets and underwent successful surgery at the Brompton Hospital. However, as a result, I lost my commercial flying licence and my employment as a pilot.

SIXTEEN

Sultan Qaboos of Oman

Especially amongst the Bedouin, it is not unusual to call a son by a surprisingly negative name. It is a very old tradition, and it is thought that the idea behind it is that the name will ward off the evil spirits as the Devil would not be interested in someone who is already harmful. An example would be 'Muatib,' meaning someone tiresome or troublesome. Another is 'Madhloom,' meaning ill-treated. 'Qaboos,' is no exception, as it means a nightmare.

Nobody could be more opposite. He was a gentle, humble, and hugely generous individual, but demanded the very highest standards from all those around him. To listen to his cut-glass English was a joy.

I shall never forget our first meeting. Shortly after my arrival, I was told that he was to inspect his new helicopter the following morning and I was to suggest the music that would be installed onto the audio system within the helicopter. That night, and with the help of an Omani friend, I spent hours researching male and female classical Arabic singers. I managed to get my friend to write a list of our suggestions in Arabic so that I could give it to the Sultan to consider. When he read the list of proposals, he thanked me and told me that his ADC would be in touch with his choices. The next morning, I was contacted and told to meet the ADC and receive my instructions. When I opened the envelope I read, 'We would prefer a library of music by Chopin, Bach, Brahms, Mozart and Prokofiev.'

I was informed by the Commander of the Royal Flight that the Sultan wished to learn to fly a helicopter and I was to give him lessons. I have the feeling that this was brought on by his close friendship with King Hussein of Jordan who was an accomplished pilot. I warned my Commander that it would entail continued instruction and that long breaks between flying lessons would have negative results, both on developing the skill and keeping up the sustained desire to fly. This turned out to be the case. After the first two or three sessions together, his duties and public commitments made the intervals between lessons longer and longer, until I was informed that he could no longer spare the time to continue. From my point of view, although this was inevitable, it was a great pity as he certainly possessed the ability and the coordination. Needless to say he was an attentive, polite, and gifted student. The most difficult manoeuvre for a student at the start is to control the helicopter in the hover - particularly in a crosswind. Qaboos held it rock steady after just thirty minutes' practice.

He was always acutely aware of how the other half lived. He was in the co-pilot's seat one morning and we were flying over the large town of Nizwa, where a picturesque section of the old town consisting of mud dwellings was being demolished to build modern accommodation. I remarked that it was a shame to destroy such beautiful and traditional houses. He turned to me and said, 'You wouldn't say that if you had to live in such unnecessary hardship.'

He did not hesitate to show his displeasure of senior members of government. During his trips from the North of the country to the South, we always knew which ministers were out of favour. We would be ordered to fly them to a small fly-infested village on the Eastern coast to spend the day amongst its discontented and vociferous inhabitants.

His greatest achievement was to take on a bankrupt, corrupt, and mediaeval country and to hoist it into a prosperous and united modern state within a decade.

SEVENTEEN

King Hussein of Jordan

Parallel with the Northern coast of Oman is a range of mountains called the Jebel Akhdar, (the Green Mountains), the highest of which is the Jebel Shams, (the Sun mountain) at around 3,000 metres above sea level. The range is famous for its labyrinth of wadis and terraced orchards, where pomegranates, apricots and roses grow. It encompasses the Saiq Plateau at 2,000m, - a flat area from which there are panoramic views.

When dignitaries flew in for audiences with the Sultan, it was common – especially during the torrid months of summer - that we flew them by helicopter to a picnic site on the Saiq Plateau to await a radio call from the palace informing us that the Sultan was ready. So in the twenty years I served Qaboos, we met and shared picnics with heads of state, prime ministers, billionaires and millionaires, and world famous celebrities. With very few exceptions they were all delightful, easy to speak with, and had fascinating personalities. However, for me, King Hussein of Jordon stood out head and shoulders above all the others.

Humble, small in stature with a film star smile he was a talented pilot. Of the many times I flew him, two occasions still remain vivid in my memory.

Omani, British, Iranian and Jordanian troops fought together in Dhofar – a mountainous area in Southern Oman - against insurgents backed by China and Russia. From June to early September the area was subjected to a benign monsoon during which the mountains were covered in mist and light rain. Overnight the arid landscape blossoms into a mass of greenery. Fighting under these conditions became difficult not only because visibility was seriously curtained, but the constant drizzle turned the trenches into mud.

King Hussein and Sultan Qaboos were close friends, and it was because of this that Jordanian troops took part in the conflict. Hussein flew in to visit his troops towards the end of one monsoon season and I landed him on a rocky area just behind the front line. His troops were in a miserable state, wet through, cold, surrounded by mud. To my amazement he got out of the helicopter and just sat down on a rock in the mist and rain by himself. After a good five minutes, a soldier passed by and, to his astonishment, recognised his Sovereign. Word spread from trench to trench and, about ten minutes later, Hussein was surrounded by a ring of seated, silent and bedraggled soldiers. Then he began to speak. It was as if he was exuding warmth and minute by minute the soldiers' hunched backs straightened, their eyes lightened as if they were physically uplifted. At the end as one they rose and cheered, and cheered, and cheered.

The second occasion was quite different. On a year when the Gulf Co-operation Council meeting was held in Muscat all the Heads of the member States were flown in one by one, some arriving the night before, and some on the day itself. Although Jordan was not an official member of the Council, King Hussein was invited to attend. On the morning of the meeting I flew him onto the parade ground. The Guard of Honour were lined up and the military band were poised to play the Jordanian National Anthem.

After landing, I quickly got out of the helicopter, ran around to open the passenger door and stood to attention ready to salute as Hussein descended the passenger steps. As he passed, he brushed my shoulder causing my epaulette to fall onto the ground. The band started the Jordan anthem, the Guard of Honour started to present arms as the king started to walk towards them. After three or four paces he stopped, turned around, returned to me, bent down, picked up the epaulette, shook my hand and then returned to the waiting reception. The band and Guard of Honour were totally confused as to what was happening. Some stopped and restarted playing, the officer in charge of the Guard of Honour turned to see what going on and – for a second or two - bewilderment reigned.

As was well known, the king was a talented fixed-wing and helicopter pilot and certainly flew the helicopter a lot better than I.

EIGHTEEN

Tail Rotor Failure on a Cliff Face

As the blades of a helicopter turn, torque is set up between them and the main fuselage below. Unless something is done, the fuselage would start to rotate in the opposite direction to the rotors. The role of the tail rotor is to stop this from happening.

Thus if, for some reason, the tail rotor stops operating the fuselage will start to spin so rapidly that, in most cases, it is impossible to control. The higher the power required at the time, the higher is the speed of rotation. In the hover a large amount of power is required.

A new naval base was to be opened by the Sultan Qaboos at the entrance to the bay of Muscat. The Sultan had invited a number of guests, which included the British Ambassador, to watch the ceremonies from his Muscat palace.

I received orders the night before to pick up twelve or so soldiers with their machine guns from the Royal Guard and drop them off at various points on the mountains overlooking the bay prior to the arrival of the Sultan.

With the full load I came to the hover at the highest point for the first drop-off on top of a cliff, directly opposite and in full view of the Sultan and his guests – and suffered a tail rotor failure. The helicopter spun violently, hit rock and started to roll down the mountainside. Half way to the sea, the helicopter came to a rest upside down in a crevice and started to burn.

I tried to reach my harness release but was unable to do so, as my full body weight was on the release mechanism. I heard the crack of ammunition exploding and realised that there was nothing I could do but wait for the flames to reach me. Bizarrely, I remember thinking that the first to burn would be my hair. Then something extraordinary occurred. An overpowering and deep, deep calm took over my mind and I knew that I would be able to bear the pain before I died. I have often wondered since whether those who were burnt at the stake who appeared so calm experienced the same phenomena.

As the back of the helicopter burned, she settled and my weight shifted in the straps so that I was able to reach and turn the release system.

Very sadly, one soldier was thrown clear and died as the helicopter rolled over him. I got away just a broken leg and cuts to my back, and was able to be flying again a month later.

NINETEEN

Arif the Thief

When I joined the Royal Flight Oman it consisted of two fixed-wing aeroplanes, - a VC10 and a Falcon together with a white Bell 212 VIP helicopter for the Sultan's use, and a 'Hughey' helicopter for escorting soldiers of the Royal Guard.

The organisation was commanded by a Polish ex-RAF fighter pilot – a delightful and hugely energetic leader. All employees lived in an accommodation complex opposite the airport, which was still being built when I arrived. The contract which I signed in the U.K. stated that we were entitled to house help. We were all accompanied and a number of the families had small children. When we asked about how we were to go about finding house help, we were told to go down to the prison in which illegal immigrants were being held and we would be allocated one of the inmates. When we arrived the individuals were already ear-marked. A small tailor from Pakistan called Arif had been allocated to my family.

His story was tragic. He had sold his family tailoring business in order to do the pilgrimage to Mecca. He was boarded onto a crowded boat and when it had arrived within five hundred meters off the coast, the passengers were told that they had arrived at the holy city and that they were to swim for shore. Arif told me that some were unable to swim. In fact, they had been discarded off the coast of Oman and, those who had made it to the beach, were immediately picked up by the police, arrested, transported to the capital area and imprisoned. He could not have been a greater help, and became invaluable to look after the house while I was away accompanying the Sultan either in Salalah, or on one of his visits abroad. Arif used to do all the food shopping and I authorised him to put household items on my account in the local shop. This went on for a year or two and I relied upon him more and more as we became busier and busier.

After Dawn and I married, I told her to carry on as I had done and leave everything to Arif. One afternoon she told me that that morning she had come back to the house early and found in the kitchen five or six bottles of cooking oil, ten packets of eggs and some cleaning cloths. She then went to the store to discover why my household expenses had been so high over the years. Arif had taken so much that he had opened a small shop in his quarters supplied solely by yours truly.

The authorities wanted to imprison him immediately, but luckily I was able to persuade them that it would be cheaper and much less trouble for him to be deported back to Pakistan. I accompanied the police escort taking him to the airport and noticed that his third suitcase was an old one that I had thrown away months before. When it was opened it was full of items taken from our house that very morning.

I was told later that soon after his return to Pakistan, he built an impressive house for himself and family.

TWENTY

A Real Mystery

My last flight before leaving the Army was a short trip to hand deliver a document to the commanding officer of a unit in Northern Germany. It was a beautiful day with not a cloud in the sky and I planned to be back within the hour. It would be a nice easy flight and I decided to take my time and savour every moment.

I arrived overhead the barracks and looked for the helipad with no success. Not only that, but there was a profusion of wires and aerials throughout the entire complex. The only possible place to land safely was a large open space surrounded by a high wire fence.

I flew low over the area and saw that there was a gate, which would allow egress. I reasoned that even if it was locked, the noise of the helicopter landing would be enough to alert the gate to be opened. The only alternative open to me was to land well outside the complex and leave the helicopter unattended while I found and delivered the package to the correct person.

My helicopter required that, immediately prior to closing the engine after a flight, the procedure was to bring the throttle back to idle for a full minute. While the engine was at idle, I looked down to put away my map and tidy the cockpit. When the time came to shut down the engine I looked outside the helicopter to see myself surrounded by five huge soldiers in military police uniform, each holding a straining Alsatian. I could see that all the dogs were barking frantically and, if freed, would certainly attack.

As soon as the rotors had stopped, my door was opened and, as my legs swung out to exit, I was grabbed under each arm and, with my feet hardly touching the ground, was almost carried towards a building, which was clearly the headquarters.

It is the only time in my life that, as I approached doors, they were opened for me.

Behind a large desk sat a moustached brigadier. After a long pause he looked up and said, 'We have safeguarded the area in every possible way and at enormous expense but never dreamt that we would have to cope for a complete imbecile as yourself. Now get out!'

I handed him the letter and was escorted almost at the run back to my helicopter.

Clearly in deep trouble, I expected a report was winging its way to my boss and that, on arrival back at base, I would face punishment.

I never heard anything more about the incident and, since that day, have no idea what was so special about that fenced area.

TWENTY-ONE

A Radical Change of Plan – Damascus

A Radical Change of Plan – Damascus

The Sultan of Oman and King Hussein of Jordan were very great friends and, possibly the fact that King Hussein was an excellent helicopter pilot, moved the Sultan to inform my chief pilot that he wished to learn how to fly helicopters.

During one of our times together, I told him how difficult it was for me to understand what was happening on the ground when we were escorting him from the air, since all the security communications were in Arabic. The next thing I knew was that I was told to take unpaid leave for six months to learn the language properly.

The natural place to go to was Jordan since both Royal Courts were closely allied and communications between the two were excellent. I chose a well-known school in Amman and booked my flight.

The evening before I travelled, I was invited to dinner with a friend and sitting opposite to me at the table was the Cultural Attaché to the British Embassy. I was very excited at the prospect of my travel the following day and told him how much I was looking forward to it. Instead of enthusing, he said that I should seriously think of changing my plans and to go somewhere else - even at this late stage.

When asked why, he replied that should I go to Jordan to learn Arabic everyone would want to answer me in English and that the learning process will be much too slow. He went on to say that I should go somewhere where the British were not popular and that English was rarely spoken. 'Where?' I asked him. 'Syria,' was the reply.

At that time Hafez al Assad was at his most bloody. However, that evening I changed my ticket and flew to Damascus. I arrived as a forty-year-old hardly speaking a word of Arabic, knowing no one and asking around for a school I could join. Of course I was immediately labelled with huge suspicion and soon after my arrival I realised that I had become of interest to the security authorities. The same gentleman in a black leather jacket seemed to appear wherever I went.

I discovered that I could only remain in Syria if I was able to enrol in a school supported by the ruling Baath party. I traced the only one, which was in an old nunnery close to the centre of the city. The headmaster made it clear that he would only allow me to enrol if I paid up front (I suspect at a highly inflated rate) and that I would be on strict probation.

The school was brilliantly organised since every class contained only one student of any particular nationality. In front of me was a Russian, and on each side there was an East German student and one from Eritrea. Thus we had no common language and were all forced to use what little Arabic we knew to communicate one with another.

It was winter and bitterly cold. The only heating was a small oil burning stove in the basement. I felt particularly miserable, as the teachers were clearly told to make my life difficult and I was forced to read articles from the newspaper, which attacked Israel and the West. The invasion of the Falkland Islands took place while I was there and this was a wonderful opportunity to humiliate me.

I began to realise that the whole adventure was a disaster and that it was almost a certainty that I would have to return to Oman admitting failure.

I was saved by something which was nothing short of a miracle: the arrival of my future wife. An American, Dawn was a Fulbright scholar teaching Anthropology at the University of Damascus in Arabic and was auditing the class lessons. Hugely talented, she was some years later to become a Professor of Anthropology teaching at the University of Oxford and a Fellow of the British Academy.

Dawn introduced me to a wonderful group of her Syrian friends and together we travelled all over that beautiful country at weekends.

We savoured the Crusade castles, St. Simeon, Roman mosaics at Kanawaat, mountain restaurants at Safita, the covered Roman market of Aleppo, the ruins of Tadmor, the museums and, above all, the hospitality and kindnesses we received wherever we went.

Once the school realised that I was there for the language and for no other reason, attitudes completely changed and I could not have felt more welcome.

Of course there was always the dark side of Syria lurking in the background. And every now and then one was suddenly faced with it.

A member of our group disappeared one day for nearly three years. He was eventually released from prison a skeleton of a man. The reason for his incarceration? He gave a party in his house and one of his guests had reported that he had a Marxist book in one of his bookshelves. As long as you never, ever discussed politics – even within the family – you were left alone. Ignore this basic rule and retribution was swift and deadly.

There appeared to be no shame on the part of the Government about making reprisals upon its citizens. The public buses travelling north were all deliberately diverted so that they had to travel through Hama in order that travellers could see what would happen to any opposition to Government. Reportedly 20,000 people were massacred. American Foreign Affairs analyst, Robin Wright, described the attack as 'the single deadliest act by any Arab government against its own people in the modern Middle East.'[1]

I shall never forget the silence as all passenger conversation ceased during the time our bus passed through the devastated city.

The market was at its highest four feet and the poor were existing amongst the ashes and open to the air.

When I returned to Oman six months later, I found that my salary had been continued.

---

[1] Danin, Robert M. "Remembering the Hama Massacre." February 2, 2012. Web. 16 October, 2021.

Dawn and I returned three or four times in later years to visit and to continue our language studies. We shall always be grateful for the warmth and kindness we received from all those we met in that beautiful country.

TWENTY-TWO

An Incompetent Enemy - San'aa, Yemen

Having lost my commercial flying licence due to a heart problem, I decided to start my own business initiating contracts between the Arab world and western companies, as well as facilitating negotiations between the two. Initially I concentrated on Oman, Syria, and Yemen.

My wife Dawn, backed and encouraged me but, wisely, persuaded me to invest only a fixed amount of capital into the company. We agreed that if the company was not making a healthy profit by the time the capital had been expended, then we would call it a day. Unfortunately, the flash to bang was too slow. Air travel to and from the Arab world, hotels, meals, transport and a hundred other expenses were too great to cope with delayed payments I received from both Arab and Western companies. The company lasted just over a year.

During one trip to Yemen, I was staying in the beautiful capital of San'aa and had to visit by taxi a potential client, who lived a mile or so outside the city. I recognised from his accent that my taxi driver, Ahmed, came from the South of the country - probably Aden. He confirmed this was correct and asked me whether I had visited the area. Feeling a little shame-faced I admitted I had taken part in the war. 'Oh,' he replied. 'so was I.'

It was a very hot day and Ahmed suggested we stop at a roadside café. As soon as we sat down I asked him in what area had he fought and what was his role. He informed me that he was in the mountainous Habalain area and his task was to mine and lay booby-traps on some of the isolated mountain helicopter pads. I asked him whether he could remember on which ones. When he told me I replied that I had landed many times on some of them and, over a cup of sweet tea together, we agreed that clearly he hadn't been too successful.

For the rest of my stay and until I arrived at the airport Departures he insisted on driving me free of charge, even refusing to take a tip when we eventually parted company.

I came away from Yemen with a feeling of great sadness. The natural fertility of the land, which can support a myriad of crops and fruit is so often misused for the cultivation of 'Qatt' – a mild sedative, which has the advantage of being an instant cash crop since it can be harvested all the year round. On top of this, the political differences between the North and the South of the country gave all the signs of being irreconcilable, foretelling – to say the least - an unhappy future.

TWENTY-THREE

Short Takes

A relation of mine was renowned throughout the Cotswolds as an expert in port. He was often asked out to dinner specifically to be tested, to identify the vineyard and year of the most obscure vintages. Throughout the years it was well-known that he only made one big mistake of which, his host at the time was proud to boast. On this occasion, he not only got the vineyard incorrect, but was wildly out with regards to the year. Other than that one incident, his record was spotless. Just before his death, I asked him for an explanation of his now celebrated error. He told me that it was the only time he was unable to access the kitchen to slip the cook a note in return for being allowed to see the bottle, which was to be served at the end of the meal.

I was tasked to fly Nelson Rockefeller and his family on a sight-seeing tour of the mountains above Muscat, prior to his audience with the Sultan of Oman. I was warned by a friend, who claimed to know of him, that he would be a difficult passenger and that I should be particularly subservient.

It was planned that immediately his executive jet landed at Seeb Airport, the party would transfer into the helicopter to do the tour. Myself, the co-pilot and crewman stood by the stairs of the helicopter expecting the passengers to board our helicopter, paying no attention to the crew. But to our amazement he and his wife stopped, shook our hands and spent about five or so minutes chatting to us all. After take-off, I remarked to my co-pilot of my surprise as to finding him so different from the person I expected. I ended by saying what a charming and delightful person he was. As he disembarked at the end of the tour he turned to me and said, 'Your charming and delightful passenger thanks you for a memorable flight.' I discovered that my crewman had mistakenly left a pair of headphones in the passenger compartment, and Rockefeller had listened to the conversation between myself and my co-pilot throughout the entire flight.

One of the illusions, which is a well-known danger at night to helicopter pilots is called the 'Black Hole Effect.' It is when the lights of the landing area are surrounded by total blackness. This can happen when the threshold lights of an airfield or oil rig are surrounded by jungle, sea or desert. On a visual approach the illusion tricks the pilot to think his or her helicopter is higher than it is in reality. This causes the approach to be to a point short of the lights and the helicopter flying into the ground. It is so powerful an illusion, that even knowledge of its danger may not be enough. A vivid example of this I remember, was picking up a survivor on a mountain at night and the only aid I had was the torch he was shining to show me his location. I kept on saying to myself 'Keep high, keep high!' but still I had to pull the helicopter up sharply at the last moment. I shall never forget watching a helicopter approaching an oilrig in the Arabian Gulf one night and its descent into the sea about a hundred metres short of the rig.

I was not a very successful officer cadet at Sandhurst and was always in and out of trouble.

One of the worst punishments that was imposed on miscreants was called 'Restrictions,' which involved being confined to barracks and having to do daily extra drills, including over the weekends. We were issued with special belts and straps, which had to be kept white with 'Blanco' (a white paste), and brass fittings. One speck of dirt on the white belt, or white Blanco on the brass, automatically involved extra days on 'Restrictions.' I was often joined by a fellow cadet who became a wonderful friend. I remember weekend after weekend with myself and Michael being screamed at by a delirious drill sergeant, while we marched sweating in splendid isolation on the enormous drill square in front of the main building. Fifteen or so years later, Michael was to become a millionaire having started with a vegetable stand in Coventry Gardens London.

One of the most terrifying people I have met was the colonel to the regiment I joined, as a new and very green young officer. I

was welcomed by the senior Subaltern who could not have been kinder. He gave me a tour of the barracks and gave me a long brief of how I was to fit into the organisation, and what was expected of me. At lunch, he told me that I had to meet the commanding officer at three o'clock that afternoon and was to report to the adjutant five minutes earlier. On time, I knocked at the door of the adjutant's office and the immaculate officer, with a wave, told me to stand outside the colonel's door until summoned. Eventually the call came and there, behind an enormous desk, was a very large gentleman with a huge white moustache. He looked up and barked 'Mylne – I note you have a car. Do you have a horse?' I replied that I did not. 'Come back when you have one!' came the response. I have never discovered whether or not he was being serious.

A revenge, which was both apt and original, happened to a well-known and hated bully at school. Amongst his victims was one he particularly tormented who was from Milan and who became a good friend. At the end of a winter term and before he travelled to Italy, he told me that he was going to get his own back on his persecutor. I asked him how, but received no answer except, 'You'll see!' On the first day of the next term he said to me, 'Just watch him' – which I did and saw a complete change of behaviour of the tyrant. He had a permanently pale and haunted look, kept to himself and reverted to an introvert. At last my friend told me the reason. In Milan he had bought a couple of pills that, if put in a drink, turned the urine of the drinker black.

Any helicopter can only lift a limited weight and, if overloaded, can lead to catastrophic results. A helicopter's performance decreases with altitude and in hot and humid conditions. Supporting the oil rigs in the Arabian Gulf, we were operating as a single pilot crew with no crewman, where temperatures were sometimes close to 40 degrees centigrade with a relative humidity in the nineties. Landing on an Italian oil rig, I was to pick up some equipment belonging to the Schlumberger company and to transfer it to an installation which had become inoperative, and which was situated about forty miles away. Every minute a rig is out of order incurs enormous losses for its company. Transfer by boat was considered to take too long, so it was vital that the flight took place. Four massive roustabouts (rig workers) struggled to lift the load into the helicopter and, concerned, I asked as to its weight. I was shown a completed load statement on which was written a weight that it was just within the helicopter's limits. To take off I pulled full power and the helicopter went nowhere. It couldn't even hover. I learnt a very valuable lesson never to trust what is written on pieces of paper, and to supervise the weighing of cargo personally, even though it might incur delays.

King Carlos of Spain was to visit Sultan Qaboos of Oman, and his private jet was due to touch down at the national airport at Seeb just before midday. Preparations were duly made for his reception, roads were prepared to be closed and all the security arrangements were in place a good hour before the expected arrival. A message was received that the flight was delayed by two hours. This was very strange as we knew that the aeroplane had taken off on time from Spain and that the flight was direct. On talking to the pilot later that day, he admitted that they had mistakenly landed at Amman in Jordan instead of Oman.

I admired him for being so honest.

I was due to take the king to a picnic site on the high mountains over-looking the coast and five minutes flying time from the Palace, prior to his audience with the Sultan. Just prior to boarding the helicopter, he said that he would like to sit up front in the cockpit with me. My co-pilot was a little put out, but refusal would have been very embarrassing. The helicopter was equipped with dual controls, so I decided to treat him as if he was one of my students. It turned out that King Carlos could fly the helicopter extremely well.